A message to parents from

Johnson's®

The most precious gift in the world is a new baby. To your little one, you are the centre of the universe. And by following your most basic instincts to touch, hold and talk to your baby, you provide the best start to a happy, healthy life.

Our baby products encourage parents to care for and nurture their children through the importance of touch, developing a deep, loving bond that transcends all others.

Parenting is not an exact science, nor is it a one-size-fits-all formula. For more than a hundred years, Johnson & Johnson has supported the healthcare needs of parents and healthcare professionals, and we understand that all parents feel more confident in their role when they have information they can trust.

That is why we offer this book as our commitment to you to provide scientifically sound, professionally reviewed guidance on the important topics of pregnancy, babycare and child development.

As you read through this book, the most important thing to remember is this: you know your baby better than anyone else. By watching, listening and having confidence in your natural ability, you will know how to use the information you have in your hands, for the benefit of the baby in your arms.

potty training

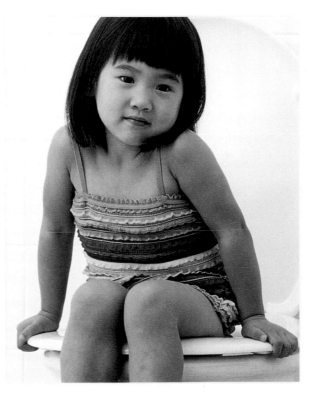

London, New York, Munich, Melbourne, Delhi

Text by Tracey Godridge
For Cora, Eden and Noah

Senior editors Julia North, Salima Hirani
Senior art editor Hannah Moore
Project editor Angela Baynham
Project art editor Alison Tumer
DTP designer Karen Constanti
Production controller Heather Hughes
Managing editors Anna Davidson, Liz Coghill
Managing art editor Glenda Fisher
Photography art direction Sally Smallwood
Photography Ruth Jenkinson

Publishing director Corinne Roberts

First published in Great Britain in 2004 by
Dorling Kindersley, A Penguin Company
80 Strand, London, WC2R 0RL

Every effort has been made to ensure that the information contained in this book is complete and
accurate. However, neither the publisher nor the author are engaged in rendering professional advice or
services to the individual reader. The ideas, procedures and suggestions contained in this book are not
intended as a substitute for consulting with your healthcare provider. All matters regarding the health of
you and your baby require medical supervision. Neither the author nor the publisher shall be liable or
responsible for any loss or damage allegedly arising from any information or suggestion in this book.

A CIP catalogue record for this book is available from the British Library

ISBN 1 4053 0437 5

Reproduced by Colourscan, Singapore
Printed by Star Standard, Singapore

See our complete catalogue at
www.dk.com

Contents

" I didn't even **start to think** about potty training until my son was two and a half. Then, once we took the plunge, he was **dry in days.** "

ELSPETH, mum to Max aged three

1

Your toddler's development

You know your toddler is growing up when she makes the big step out of nappies into pants. But this won't happen until her brain is developed enough to control her bowel and bladder – any time between 18 and 36 months – and she has reached a certain level of emotional and physical maturity.

The physical basics

You can probably hardly wait to introduce your toddler to the potty, especially after months of nappy changing. A life without nappies will be lighter on your workload as well as on your pocket! But until she is physically and emotionally ready there's nothing you can do to speed up the process.

Until now your toddler has emptied her bladder and bowel automatically as a reflex action whenever they have felt full. She will begin to be aware that she's doing a wee or a poo only when the nerve pathways from her bladder and bowel to her brain have fully matured. This usually happens at around 18 months of age.

Even then she still won't be able to predict when she needs to empty her bowels and bladder – it will be some time before she's familiar with the feelings of needing to go and has developed the physical control to hang on. This usually happens by about two and a half years, although it can be earlier or later.

Mastering new skills

Gaining a sense of bowel and bladder control is an exciting step forward. But your toddler also needs to be willing and able to cope with the mechanics of using a potty. As with all new skills, your toddler will master potty training in her own way and at her own speed. Some toddlers – usually the older ones – become potty trained very quickly and rarely have an accident, while the majority have false starts and setbacks along the way.

Getting ready

Your toddler needs a variety of physical, verbal and emotional skills before she is ready for potty training.
- **Ability to "hang on"** If your child is managing a reasonable amount of time during the day without doing a wee then she is probably developing some control over her bladder. Potty training isn't really practical if she's wetting her nappy every hour or so. You can check to see how frequently she's weeing by checking her nappy. If it's still dry after a couple of hours then that is a good first step.
- **Awareness of what she's doing** Watch her face – she may stop playing, stand still, look at you, go red in the face and even try to tell you what's happening.

> ### Expert tip
>
> When it comes to potty training there's a strong genetic link. So if you want any clues as to when your child is likely to be ready, it may be worth asking your parents about your own performance as a toddler.

Is my toddler ready for potty training?

Only your toddler can tell you whether or not she's ready for potty training. She won't use words – but watch her closely and you should be able to spot the tell-tale signs. Lots of toddlers reach this stage some time between 18 and 24 months – but many others aren't ready until some months later.

Spotting the signs

You'll be thinking about potty training some time around your toddler's second birthday. But is she thinking about it too? There are many different signs that show your child may be ready to start – here's a checklist to help work out whether or not now is a good time to get started:

★ your child stays dry at least two hours at a time during the day or is dry after naps

★ her bowel movements are fairly regular

★ her nappy is often dry – this shows she can last a period of time without weeing

★ she's aware when she's doing a wee or a poo

★ she's reasonably coordinated so can sit comfortably on the potty and pull her pants up and down

★ she's interested in what happens when you go to the toilet.

"WHAT ARE YOU DOING, MUM?"
If your child seems interested in what is going on when you use the toilet, then this is a good sign that she will be ready to start potty training soon.

A NEED FOR INDEPENDENCE

As your little one gets older she will want more independence. If she is trying to do things such as fastening up her coat for herself, you can begin to start thinking about potty training.

FOLLOWING INSTRUCTIONS

Being able to follow simple instructions – passing you something when you ask her to, for example – is another sign that your child is ready for potty training.

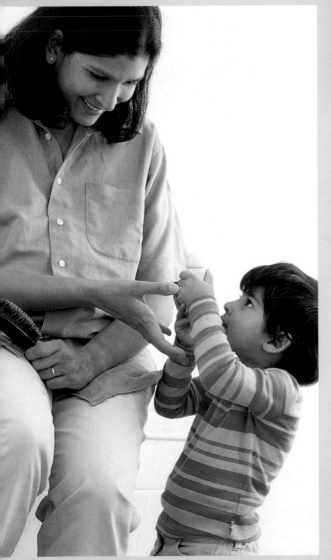

Other signs of nearing readiness include:

★ she can follow simple instructions

★ she's keen to do things for herself

★ she's eager to please and imitate you

★ she shows a desire for independence.

You don't need to be able to tick off every item in this checklist to start potty training but, before you take the plunge, your toddler should know she's doing a poo or wee, and show an interest in being like a "grown-up".

Your toddler is not ready if:

★ she's under 18 months old

★ she has no idea what's happening when she does a wee or a poo

★ she isn't interested in imitating you

★ she's resistant to being told what to do.

Expert tips

Even if your toddler isn't ready to start using a potty it's worth introducing the subject in a low-key way:

● when you change her nappy use words such as "poo" and "wee"

● stay matter of fact – not critical – about the state of her nappies

● discourage older children from making any negative comments about dirty nappies

● let her see you using the loo.

"When Alex was about two and a half he started to become aware of when he was doing a wee or a poo and would often come and tell me. I quickly realized the time had arrived when he was ready to take the big step out of nappies and into pants."

SUZANNE, mum to Alex, now three

If she has no clothes on and is looking at the puddle she has made and clutching herself, then she's also connecting the feeling she has with what has happened.

NAPPY CHECK
Noting how often your child's nappy is wet will give you some idea as to when she is ready to start potty training.

● **Coordination** Very young children and those who were later learning to crawl and walk may have problems arranging themselves on a potty as well as finding pulling their pants up and down tricky. Knocking a potty over or struggling with clothes will inevitably be upsetting for your child and frustrating for you.

● **Understanding of what you tell her** By two years old, most toddlers are saying their first words and they may have the words "poo" or "wee" (or whichever you choose to use) already in their vocabulary. Even if your toddler isn't talking much yet, it's a huge help if she can understand what you are saying when, for example, you show her a potty and explain what it is for. Being able to follow simple instructions such as "let's find your potty" will also help her grasp what's needed and when.

Questions & Answers

Do boys take longer than girls?
Lots of mums say that their daughters were out of nappies earlier than their sons – and, on the whole, girls do seem to master potty training before boys. Boys, for example, appear to be less interested than girls at the same age, and tend to have accidents up to a later age than girls. This could be to do with their language skills – girls are often more keen to communicate at this age, and success at potty training depends to a certain extent on understanding language and being able to respond to it. Potty training isn't a race – and it's worth remembering that the toddler who starts later often gets there faster!

My mother says I was potty trained by 18 months. Could this be true?
In the days before disposables, when nappies were washed by hand, mums were keen to get their toddlers "dry" as quickly as possible. However, it's likely it was more to do with good timing than training. Figuring out when your child is likely to need a poo – after a meal, for example – and then sitting her on the potty until she does one, may teach her what her potty is for but not how to control her bowel movements. True potty training is when you give your toddler the chance to recognize for herself when she needs to empty her bowel or bladder – and she can only do this when she is developmentally ready.

• **Willingness to try** Around 18 months, when toddlers experience a surge of independence, difficult behaviour is common. Refusing to cooperate over even the simplest task is entirely normal for a child this age. Coping with resistance from your toddler can be challenging at the best of times. Rather than put your toddler – or yourself – under any extra pressure, wait for a time when she's feeling less negative.

Making the right decision
Social pressure to potty train your toddler before she's ready can be intense. Maybe your friend's son is the same age and is out of nappies already and you're worried that your daughter should be too. Perhaps you are expecting another

STAY POSITIVE
Avoid negative comments about the state of your child's nappies when you change them.

SUMMER FUN
Warm sunny days provide a great opportunity for your child to get used to spending time without her nappy on.

Children with special needs

Mastering potty training is a major achievement for all children – and those with special needs especially benefit from this step towards independence. It can, however, take a lot longer for a child with physical or learning difficulties and will certainly involve a much greater degree of patience and understanding. Children who have hearing problems, for example, will find communication harder; those with coordination problems will find coping with clothes and sitting on a potty difficult.

If your child has special needs you may find expert help is useful in judging the right time to start and the best way of teaching bowel and bladder control. Charities and self-help groups can offer useful information on this subject and will be able to put you in touch with other parents who can share their experiences with you. Your GP or health visitor is also a good starting point.

baby and feel life with a newborn would be easier if your oldest child was out of nappies. Or maybe your parents are making you feel guilty that your child isn't potty trained yet – 40 years ago early potty training was much more popular.

When it comes to giving up nappies, however, there's only one timetable that matters to your toddler and that's her own. Try to remember that your toddler has a better chance of success if you wait until she's clearly ready. Meanwhile, explain to friends and family the approach you are taking and ask for their support.

Going at her pace

There's little point in trying to potty train your toddler before she has reached the required stages of development (see pages 8–9). Starting too soon will at best result in lots of puddles and soiled pants, at worst your toddler will become upset, possibly resistant, and the whole process will take a lot longer.

Like crawling and walking, potty training is a developmental task that your toddler will be ready for at her own pace. And whether she gets there earlier or later has no connection with her intelligence or other areas of development. For example, a child who was slow to crawl won't necessarily be older when she's ready for potty training; and similarly a child who is out of nappies at a younger age won't necessarily be an early reader.

The best route to success is to follow your child's lead. After all, there's no hurry – and, as with acquiring all new skills, your toddler will get there in her own time. Being patient and waiting for signs of readiness and willingness helps pave the way for earlier success – which in turn will give your toddler a real confidence boost.

Potty training twins

If you are the parent of twins – and dealing with a double quota of nappies – there may be an extra temptation to hurry potty training. As with singletons, however, starting your twin toddlers before they are ready could backfire. Coping with double the number of wet pants and puddles can't be any better than changing extra nappies.

It's possible that one of your twins will be ready before the other, as all children – even twins – develop at different rates. Seeing a sibling's progress may spur the other one along in the right direction. But don't forget that potty training isn't a competition – either between the children in your family or between peers. If one toddler is interested before the other, try to encourage and praise in a low-key way. Even if your other twin appears to be totally uninterested, hearing her brother or sister applauded for something she can't - or doesn't want to – do may create tension and cause unnecessary setbacks.

TWINS IN TRAINING
Allowing each toddler to reach his individual developmental milestones will help prevent potty training becoming a competition between them.

Starting later

The likelihood is that the later you leave potty training, the easier it will be. Studies have shown, for example, that many children who begin potty training before they are 18 months aren't completely trained until after the age of four; whereas those who don't start until after their second birthday are completely trained by the time they reach the age of three.

When is the best time to start potty training?

The best time to start encouraging your toddler in this new skill is when she is showing signs of readiness and has a settled and happy routine. Any disruptive event in your toddler's life could cause a setback in her behaviour and make it a bad time to consider potty training.

Starting at the right time

You know your child best and can tell how much change or stress she can cope with. But if there are upheavals in her life, it makes sense to wait until her routine is back to normal, or at least more settled. Making even gentle demands on a child who's coping with disruption can cause distress and be unsuccessful.

Rain or shine?

Lots of mums start potty training when the weather is fine and their toddlers can run around lightly dressed – or, better still, not dressed at all. Your child will undoubtedly have a better chance of making it to the potty on time if she doesn't have to strip off layers of clothes first. But whatever

EASY DRESSING
If your toddler starts potty training in the summer then wearing less clothing will help her to master new skills.

the weather, if your toddler shows all the signs of being ready, that's the time to start teaching her – even if it's in the middle of winter. You can, after all, keep the house a little warmer so she can at least wear less when she's indoors.

When to wait

Put off potty training if your toddler is having to deal with any of the following situations:

★ starting at playgroup

★ starting with a new childminder

★ a recent stay in hospital (you or her)

★ a house move

★ separation or divorce

★ the loss - by death or separation - of someone she was close to.

A new sibling

If you are expecting a new baby, the thought of having two in nappies may tempt you to think about potty training your toddler. But while she's getting used to sharing your attention with a new baby brother or sister, your toddler is probably going to be less cooperative than usual, at least for a while. Think about it from your point of view as well - is this the best time to be cleaning up puddles and dealing with potties while also caring for your newborn?

NEW ARRIVALS
Don't start potty training your toddler when the arrival of a new baby is imminent – give your child the chance to get used to her new sibling before you and she embark on this next step.

" Up until now Jack hasn't taken much notice of anyone using the toilet, but **looking at pictures** of other toddlers on the potty has definitely helped **stimulate his interest.** "

JOANNA, mum to Jack, 26 months

2

Preparing your toddler

Before beginning potty training you need to introduce your toddler to the potty. It's worth having one in the house from 18 months onwards. You can also start teaching him the skills he'll need for using the potty. But remember – at this age he's just becoming familiar with the whole business and is not ready to be out of nappies.

First things first

Your toddler still has a long way to go before he's ready to start routinely using the potty. But the better prepared he is now, the easier it will be when he's ready to make the change.

First he needs to know what a potty is – and what it's used for. You may already have a potty – or perhaps you could take your toddler to the shops to choose one. Having one in the house will give you the chance to explain all about it. Introducing the potty, however, needs to be done gradually and gently – too much pressure could put him off. But there are lots of fun ways of getting him interested (see page 24).

Growing up

Encouraging your toddler's sense of independence will help lay down good foundations for successful potty training. He needs to be confident about trying things on his own – and, as most toddlers are keen to be in control, now is a good time to give him lots of opportunities to be "grown-up".

Paving the way

When it comes to potty training, your goal is to make the process as positive and natural for your toddler as possible. In this way, you will stimulate his desire for independence, help him feel loved and valued – and boost your confidence as a parent too.

One of the first steps towards this goal is to make sure your toddler is well prepared. As with every new skill, learning to use a potty is a step-by-step process and your toddler needs lots of experience and opportunities to practise before he can really master it. Putting a potty in front of him and expecting him to use it when he has no concept

Potty or toilet?

Most toddlers learn how to use a potty before moving on to using the toilet. There are lots of reasons why a potty is best.

● It's portable – you can have it upstairs, downstairs, move it from room to room and whisk it under your toddler's bottom just when he needs it! You can even take it with you on shopping trips and on visits to friends or family.

● It's comfortable – generally, toddlers are happier to sit on a potty than on the toilet, which can be scary to begin with, even with a special seat on it.

● It's effective – your toddler's body is in more of a "squatting" position on a potty than on a toilet, making it easier to do a poo.

Potty hygiene

Putting a piece of loo paper in the bottom before your toddler does a poo can make dirty potties easy to clean out. Tip the contents down the loo before rinsing out. A regular wash with hot, soapy water will help prevent smells.

of what going to the toilet is, is at best likely to baffle him and at worst will create problems that may take many months to overcome.

Instead, you need to give him the chance to get used to the idea without any pressure to perform. For example, having a potty already in the bathroom and letting him see

you and your partner use the toilet, introducing the language you plan to use and making potty training as matter of fact as possible will help the change from nappies to potty progress more smoothly.

Choosing a potty

Potties today come in specially moulded plastic making them light, easy to clean and warm to sit on! When choosing which to buy, bear in mind that it should be sturdy

PRACTISING WITH DOLLY
Sitting her dolly on a potty at the same time will make the introduction of potty training even more fun for your child.

Toilet seats

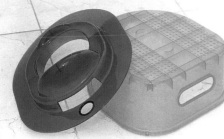

TOILET ACCESSORIES
If your child is keen to use the toilet, a child's seat and plastic step will make the experience safe and comfortable.

Your toddler may want to imitate you and use the toilet instead of a potty. Rather than discourage him, consider buying a proper child's toilet seat. For a toddler, sitting perched on the bowl of the toilet may be frightening as well as dangerous. Choose a seat that's comfortable and attaches firmly. You'll need a small, stable stool or plastic box next to the toilet, too, so your child can easily climb up to the seat. This will also help him stabilize himself with his feet while he's sitting there.

It's best to keep the seat permanently on the toilet so it's always ready when your toddler needs it. Other members of the family can simply remove it when they need to use the toilet themselves – encourage them to remember to replace it when they've finished.

and durable with a broad stable base so that it won't tip over when your toddler gets up. It should be curved inside for easy cleaning, with a moulded back support and a slot for carrying.

A basic potty is inexpensive. You can, however, spend more if you are looking for something more fun to help stimulate interest. You can choose from a wide variety, including potties moulded into different shapes such as animals and cars, musical potties, and potties that change colour when they are used.

Letting your toddler know that the potty is his is a great way of helping him feel in control. If he's interested, let him put stickers on it or print his name on it with an indelible marker.

Useful features include:
• a splash guard – this is good for boys who may have difficulty remembering to point their willy downwards – although this is no guarantee that urine won't be accidentally sprayed over the edge. Girls can still use potties with a splash guard – they just need to be taught to sit with it at the back.
• a lid – this will keep any unpleasant odours trapped, which helps at other people's houses and when carrying and emptying the potty. If you are out in the car, a lid also

FUN FEATURES
Potties which are bright colours or fun shapes will help to stimulate your toddler's interest in potty training.

How do I introduce the potty?

Introducing the potty to your toddler is the first step towards potty training. The best time to do this is at about 18 months. Having a potty in the house is all about getting your toddler used to seeing it around and giving you the chance to talk about what it's for. Remember that at this stage your toddler is still not ready to start potty training.

Choose a spot

The best place for your toddler's potty is close to the family toilet. This will help her make the association between going to the toilet and using the potty. If, however, she wants to move it around the house then let her: feeling that the potty is under her control will help motivate her sense of independence.

Toddlers love to imitate, so it helps if you feel relaxed about using the toilet with her around. Going to the toilet together will also help give you the chance to talk about what's happening and help her make the right connections.

Practice makes perfect

Whenever you can, encourage your toddler to sit on the potty. To begin with she may just want to explore it and play with it, but after a while she'll start to sit on it. At first she may do this only with her clothes on, but once she has practised a few times you can suggest she tries with her nappy off.

If she enjoys sitting there, let her have a go whenever she likes. The more familiar she is with her potty the happier she'll be to use it when the time comes.

GETTING FAMILIAR
Allowing your child to play games with her new potty gets her familiar with it, as well as creating the opportunity to talk about what it's for.

POTTY PLAY
Letting your toddler sit on her potty whenever she wants to will make her happier to use it when the time for potty training arrives.

Once your toddler has become used to the potty, try to make it part of your morning or evening routine. When she gets out of bed or before getting in the bath you could suggest she sits on the potty for a short while.

Be patient

Initially your toddler may show no interest in the potty or resist being asked to have a go at sitting on it. If this is the case, don't push her. As the months go by a little gentle encouragement may do no harm, but for now it's best to leave her until she feels properly ready.

If she does do a wee or a poo, show her that you are pleased but don't get overexcited – too much praise might put her under pressure to perform again and at this age she may choose to give up on the potty altogether rather than risk not getting your applause. It's early days and it was probably good timing rather than a sign to start potty training.

LIKE A "GROWN UP"
Give your child lots of praise when she does helpful things such as putting her toys away – this will boost her confidence and sense of independence.

means you can safely keep a used potty in the car boot until you reach somewhere it can be emptied.

Potty vocabulary

Potty training will be easier for your toddler if the same words are used by everyone in the house, and your toddler is already familiar with them. Which words you choose will depend on your personal preference, but they should be easy for your toddler to understand and use himself.

Bear in mind, however, that there will be times when your toddler, unaware of social niceties, may use these words in public! Most people

Expert tips

● Sometimes even the most creative ideas to encourage your toddler to sit on his potty (see page 24) will fall flat if he's not ready. Rather than risk building resentment, ignore any mention of the potty until your toddler starts to show real interest himself.

● Never force your toddler to sit on the potty – getting cross or physically restraining him won't accomplish anything. In fact, it will have quite the opposite effect – your toddler will become fearful and may resist the potty altogether for many months.

are not offended by the words "poo" or "wee" and you will probably find this is the vocabulary your health visitor and GP use.

As your toddler gets older, you can teach him to say "I need the loo please" as an acceptable alternative to describing exactly what he needs it for!

Nurturing independence

Encouraging your toddler to be independent will help build his confidence and give him just the boost he needs to handle the change from nappies to potty. Toddlers are naturally keen to be in control and do things for themselves – even when they can't always manage! But the more your toddler can do for himself the happier he'll be.

● **Let him have a go** Your toddler loves showing you how clever he is and your enthusiasm is always the best reward when he tries something new – even if he finds it difficult to master at first.

● **Give him lots of praise** This is especially important when he behaves in a "grown-up" way, whether it's putting his toys away or using his fork properly.

● **Have realistic expectations** All children develop at different rates, so don't compare your toddler with others. Instead, watch him when he

POTTIES ARE FUN
Let your toddler play with toys or look at books while he sits on his potty – or better still, read his favourite book to him.

wants to do something for himself, be there for him if he needs your help but let him feel as if he's done it on his own.

Learning new skills

Helping your toddler learn how to use the potty isn't just about encouraging him to sit on one when he needs a wee or a poo. He also needs to learn a few practical skills.

● **Hand washing** Teaching your toddler good cleaning habits now will stand him in good stead when it comes to using the potty. Make hand washing part of his pre-meal routine – but encourage your toddler to do it for himself. Make sure he has easy access to a sink (a stable step-stool helps) and put the soap within reach. Liquid soap is less slippery for little fingers than bar soap.

How can I get my toddler interested in the potty?

Although some toddlers are happy to be introduced to the potty at around 18 months, others remain blissfully uninterested for a lot longer. However, there are a number of fun tactics you could use to stimulate your toddler's interest. A little low-key motivation may be all that's needed to encourage her in the right direction.

Making it fun

You have done all the right things – there's a potty in the family bathroom, you've told your toddler what it's for and encouraged her to have a go at sitting on it. But she's still not interested. What can you do? It may be worth trying the following fun ideas:

★ looking together at a fun book about potties will help prepare your toddler

★ surrounding her potty with things to look at – her favourite books or toys

★ enlisting the help of an older sibling or friend – toddlers often idolize older children, and seeing them use the toilet may make the breakthrough

★ playing games together which involve her teddies or dolls using the potty

★ watching a video with her while she sits on the potty.

Your toddler needs to associate the potty with happy moments, so even if she sits on the potty then gets up seconds later without having done anything, give her lots of praise. Remember, at this stage, you are just introducing her to the idea of the potty.

PANTS AT THE READY
Buy some "big girl" pants for your toddler. Show them to her and talk to her about what they are for. Tell her that one day, when she's ready, she'll be able to wear them.

Check the water isn't too hot and then leave him to it – the more control he has the more grown-up he'll feel.

● **Dressing and undressing** Your toddler will have much more success getting to the potty on time if he can handle the fiddly business of pulling trousers down and pants off. Give him lots of opportunities to practise getting dressed and undressed himself – even if it sometimes seems simpler and quicker to take over and do it for him. Choosing stretchy loose-fitting clothes without too many fastenings will help him manage on his own.

HYGIENIC HABITS

Making hand washing a part of your toddler's daily routine from an early age will ensure she develops good hygiene habits to last her a lifetime.

Questions & Answers

My son is nearly two and a half years old and has no interest in the potty at all. If I try to get him to sit on it he just cries. What should I do?

Nothing. He's obviously not ready for potty training, and insisting that he sits on his potty is just upsetting him and making you frustrated. He's physically and emotionally unable to cope. Put the potty away, let him forget all about it, then try again in a month or so.

My two year old always wants me to do everything for him. He won't have a go at putting on his own shoes or doing a puzzle unless I'm there to help. How will he ever be potty trained if he won't try anything for himself?

Some toddlers would rather not try to do anything at all than risk failure. He could be a natural perfectionist, or perhaps more has been expected of him than he can deliver. Make sure you are not setting unrealistic standards – this could damage his self-esteem and make him fearful of even trying. Instead, give him small things to do with you which you know he's capable of – helping to put the washing in the machine or unpack the shopping – and praise him even when he just tries. Gradually his confidence will start to grow. Meanwhile, keep potty training off the agenda until he's properly motivated.

" Martine was nearly two and a half when she first **showed any interest** in her potty. Every time she asked to use it I clapped and **sang her praises**. "

MONIQUE, mum to Martine, now three

First days out of nappies

Once your toddler is ready to begin potty training, stay calm and relaxed and things should proceed smoothly. Remember that the key point is to make using the potty seem as natural and normal as possible. With your praise – and maybe a few extra incentives – your toddler will enjoy making this big step towards independence.

A gradual process

When you feel confident that your toddler is ready to begin potty training, you need to be ready to help and encourage her. With your active support, she is likely to reach dryness without much trouble – and will be happy and confident throughout the process.

For most toddlers, learning to use the potty successfully is a step-by-step process and your toddler will progress through each stage at her own pace. Each child reaches dryness at a different age so it's important not to talk about your toddler's achievements (or lack of) with other mums or dads. Instead, be positive and remind yourself that she needs all your support and encouragement.

Ways to help

Your toddler may be grown-up enough to use a potty, but that doesn't mean she's ready to cope entirely on her own. For a while yet you'll need to be on hand to remind her, help with her clothes, check she's wiped herself properly – and even offer some small incentives when the novelty of potty training begins to wane. Giving her as much attention as possible during this phase will help her work towards success.

Trial and error

You've introduced your toddler to the potty, she enjoys sitting on it and has even had a few successes with it. She understands what it is for and is by now showing most – and maybe all – of the signs that say she's ready for potty training (see pages 8–9).

Remember that, to a large extent, learning to use the potty is all about trial and error – although some toddlers go from nappies to pants with few accidents, for others it's a slower, more gradual change.

Checklist

Once you've decided that your toddler is ready for potty training, check that you are too. You will need:

- lots of pairs of pants – there are bound to be accidents, so you need plenty of spares

- time at home – aim to start potty training during a quiet time so your toddler isn't distracted or coping with change

- a plan of action – are you going to ditch nappies from day one or start off with trainer pants (see page 29)? Think about how you are going to handle accidents – deciding now will help you be consistent

- a stash of rewards and/or incentives (see Ways to motivate, pages 34–35) – having her favourite books or videos to hand will help you when a little gentle persuasion is needed.

GOODBYE TO NAPPIES
Putting on "big boy's pants" for the first time is an exciting step towards independence for your toddler.

The important point is to make the whole process as relaxed and natural as possible.

There are different ways to go about potty training – some parents like to start their toddlers off in trainer pants (see box opposite) while others feel it's best to go straight into pants. If you can't decide which method is best for your toddler, have a chat with your health visitor. Whichever way you choose, following these suggested steps will help the first few days of potty training run smoothly.

Step one

A few days before you start potty training.

● Increase the opportunities your toddler has for sitting on the potty, especially at those key moments, such as after a meal, when she's more likely to do a poo or a wee. Never force her to stay there longer than she wants – even just a few seconds is fine.

● After the first couple of mornings or afternoons, let her run around and play for extended sessions without her nappy on. Keep a close eye on her – you might be able to tell in advance if something is about to happen!

• If she does do a wee or a poo without reaching the potty, just be matter of fact. Tell her to let you know when she's wet because then you can change her quickly so she's comfortable and dry again. Being aware that she's done a wee or poo is the first important step to recognizing she's about to do one.

Step two

On the day you decide to start.

• Put the nappies away and get out her new "big girl pants" or trainer pants (see box below). Explain to your toddler that today she doesn't need her nappy. If she can put the pants on herself, all the better –

REWARDING SUCCESS
Keep a supply of favourite treats handy to reward your child's successes.

Expert tips

Do dress your toddler in clothes she can easily manage herself. Pull-up trousers with elastic waistbands, skirts and dresses are best, whereas zips on trousers and clasps on dungarees are difficult for small fingers.

Do tell everyone who looks after your toddler that you are potty training so that they can help, too.

Don't give up too quickly – even if you have just a few successes it's worth persevering – switching back to nappies occasionally because it's more convenient may confuse your toddler.

Don't expect too much – your toddler is still getting used to "hanging on", so don't forget to take the potty with you on car journeys or shopping trips (see pages 48–51).

Disposable trainer pants

Disposable trainer pants can be pulled up and down like real pants but have the extra padding of nappies and side seams which can be torn so they can be quickly removed. Some parents use them as a half-way house but others prefer to take the plunge and do away with nappies completely.

Advantages
• Your toddler can put them on and take them off just like real pants.
• They absorb any accidents without soiling her clothes.

Disadvantages
• Your toddler won't know when she's wet – making the link between weeing and needing the potty harder.
• She may treat them just like nappies and give up trying to reach the potty altogether.

I've just started potty training my toddler. When can I expect her to be dry?

Starting potty training is an exciting moment for most parents as it brings with it the inviting prospect of life without nappies. It's also a big step forward for your child in terms of her independence. But don't rush it – the process of becoming totally dry can take some time and each child will achieve dryness at a different age, so try not to have predetermined expectations.

How it happens

Some children get the hang of using the potty within a few days - these are usually the older ones. Many more - and especially toddlers who find change difficult to handle - take several months. This is because learning to use the potty is a step-by-step process and children need lots of experience and practice in different situations before they can really master it. Here are the different stages your toddler needs to go through.

Stage one

Recognizing when she's done a wee or a poo. You can help by getting her to sit on the potty or toilet at key moments such as first thing in the morning when she wakes up or after a meal.

GOOD TIMING
Encouraging your toddler to sit on her potty or the toilet first thing in the morning when she probably needs a wee will help her to recognize when she has done one.

Stage two

Telling you she needs to go – there won't be much time between words and actions in the early days.

Stage three

Being able to "hang on". Having enough control to wait while you find the potty or a toilet can take a couple more months, as the strengthening of the bowel and bladder muscles happens gradually.

Clean and dry

Your toddler will probably discover how to stay clean – using her potty rather than her nappy for a poo – around the same time she starts to stay dry. This is because urination usually occurs with the bowel movements, so it is difficult for your toddler to differentiate between the two acts.

HANGING ON
In time, your toddler will gain the control needed to hang on while you find a toilet or potty.

TELLING YOU WHAT SHE NEEDS
Being able to tell you that she needs a wee or a poo is a major step forward in the process of potty training your toddler. Keep a potty handy to begin with as you may not get much warning.

EASY ON, EASY OFF
Dress your toddler in clothes he can easily manage. This will help him master the skills required to use the potty.

your toddler will love being so independent and grown-up.

● Remind her to ask you for her potty when she feels that she needs it – try to have it close by so she can reach it easily and quickly (one potty upstairs and one downstairs is a good idea).

● Watch the clock – if she hasn't been for while, if she had a large cup of juice an hour or so ago, or if it's around the time she usually has a poo, give her a few timely reminders.

● Encourage your toddler with lots of praise and remind her how grown-up she is.

● When she has an accident don't react negatively - just remind your toddler what the potty is for and change her without a fuss.

Working towards dryness

Don't expect too much from your toddler during these first few days out of nappies. Can you remember how she learnt to walk? It's unlikely that she just stood up and walked across the room one day. Instead she would have tottered and stumbled for many days before getting the hang of it.

As with walking, potty training is usually a gradual process. While there are toddlers – especially the older ones – who are dry from day one with hardly ever an accident, there are many more who take their time learning how to stay dry and clean. Here's what will and what won't help along the way.

"John learnt to use the potty quite quickly, but he still needs a little help now and then. He finds elasticated waistbands easiest to cope with on his own."

MIRIAM, mum to John, now three

What works

● Taking it slowly – getting to grips with the different stages of toilet training (see pages 30–31) can take a while, and your toddler will move on when she's ready.

● Lots of praise – tell your toddler that you are proud of what she's done when she tries to use her potty (even if she doesn't always manage it successfully). But don't get too excited – too much praise may make your toddler nervous and worried about failing next time, which can put her off trying.

● Staying close by – your toddler may be ready to use the potty, but she's not yet grown-up enough to cope alone.

● Expecting accidents – it's inevitable that there will be some, so don't be surprised or impatient when they happen (see page 37).

● Staying calm – when accidents do happen, simply clean up without commenting and remind your toddler to try using her potty next time.

What doesn't work

● Forcing your toddler to stay on the potty – this will simply make her frightened and much less likely to cooperate.

● Talking to others about her progress – or lack of it – in front

Daytime naps

Switching back into nappies for daytime naps may help your toddler avoid accidents but it does send mixed messages which could be confusing for her. Instead you could:

● encourage her to use her potty before putting her down for a sleep

● put a plastic cover under the sheet of her cot to protect the mattress in case she does have an accident

● if she falls asleep unexpectedly, protect the car seat, sofa or buggy with a folded towel.

NAPPY-FREE NAPS
Avoid using nappies just for daytime naps as this could confuse your toddler. Instead take precautions to minimize the mess should any accidents happen.

of her. Any sense of disappointment or impatience on your part will be picked up by your toddler.

● Putting on the pressure – your toddler will progress at her own speed, and pushing her faster than she can cope with may make her nervous and unable to poo at all.

● Punishing your toddler – if she's not interested in using the potty or has an accident, getting angry will only make matters worse.

● Showing signs of disgust – dealing with dirty potties or clearing up a

pooey accident can be unpleasant, but disdainful comments or gestures will upset your toddler.

Just for girls

Most toddlers are happy for their parents to wipe their bottoms for them and most parents are happy to do it, as getting it right can take a lot of practice. If, however, your toddler is keen to do it herself, it's important you teach her how to do it properly. Explain to her that she must move the toilet paper from the

Expert tips

Don't expect your toddler to use her potty on command. In the early days, she'll wee only when she feels the need. It won't be until she's at least three years old that you'll be able to ask her to "have a try" before going out.

Do be careful about the words you use. Avoid telling her she's a "good" girl for using the potty or a "naughty girl" for having an accident as this turns the use of the potty into a moral issue.

front of her bottom to the back, especially if she has done a poo. This is to prevent bacteria passing from her bowel to her vagina where it could cause infection.

For now, she may be happy for you to carry on wiping her bottom for her. If not, see if she will let you have the "last wipe" or a quick look to check that the job has been done properly. When she's just done a wee, a dab with the toilet paper should be sufficient to keep her dry.

"GUESS WHAT I CAN DO"
Letting your toddler telephone granny with news of his achievements will help keep him interested in his new goals.

Just for boys

Most toddlers poo and wee at the same time, so it makes sense to teach your son to sit on the potty when he's first getting the hang of potty training. Once he's happy using his potty, he may want to try standing up to wee (see page 41 for teaching tips) but even when he's graduated to the toilet, if he wants to carry on sitting he should be allowed to do so.

When it comes to bottom wiping, your son will probably be happy for you to do this for him. If not, see if you can persuade him to let you have the "last wipe" or just a check to see that the job has been done properly.

Ways to motivate

It's common for toddlers to start to lose interest in potty training. For some, lots of praise is enough to keep them going, as well as reminders about how grown-up they are. Toddlers also love feeling in control, so gradually giving her more responsibility, such as preparing the toilet paper or helping tip the potty contents down the loo then flushing it, may help keep her interested.

For others, more tangible rewards work best – as long as you avoid letting your toddler dictate the prize! It's likely that, once your toddler is on the way to being permanently dry,

she won't need these extra incentives. Keep the rewards small:

- make her a sticker chart – each time she uses her potty she can choose a sticker and put it on her chart
- let her have one of her favourite treats or a cup of her favourite juice each time she has a success
- telephoning granny or granddad to tell them about her triumphs will help her feel grown-up
- show her how magic water works – drip some blue food colouring into the toilet and your toddler will be thrilled to see the water turn green when she does a wee
- put several favourite books next to the toilet so she can read them when she has to go.

STAR PERFORMANCE
Make a chart together so your toddler can stick on a star each time she uses her potty. This will help keep her motivated.

Questions & Answers

My daughter drinks a lot during the day and I'm worried this may make potty training harder. Should I restrict the amount of fluid she has?

Cutting down on the number of drinks your toddler has during the day may help her avoid accidents but it's not good for her health. If your daughter is thirsty, she needs to drink. And in fact, needing to use the potty frequently is more likely to help her get the hang of potty training as she will have more chances to practise.

My toddler's due to start nursery in a few months time – but she's not potty trained yet. What should I do?

Nursery schools often insist that children are out of nappies before they start. But this isn't always the case – day-care nurseries, for example, which take children from a few months old, will often help with potty training. If you are planning to send your child to nursery, ask about their policy. If they would like your toddler to be dry before she starts, you will need to plan ahead and decide when to start introducing the potty. Bear in mind, however, that if your toddler simply is not ready, starting her too soon may actually slow the process.

" I quickly came to realize that **accidents** are an integral part of potty training! Whenever Lucy has one I give **her a cuddle** and reassure her she'll get it right next time. "

DAVID, dad to Lucy, nearly three

4

What to expect

Some toddlers sail through potty training with few hitches. Others seem to take two steps forward and one back. Knowing what to expect during potty training – from accidents to toilet fears – will help you support your toddler along the way, boosting his confidence and making the whole process seem entirely normal and natural.

All about accidents

Learning how to stay dry is a big step for your toddler – and understanding what's likely to happen along the way will help you tune into his needs, and respond in the best and most effective way possible.

Life is so exciting for your toddler, it's sometimes easy for him to forget about using the potty. Accidents are entirely natural – especially when you first start – and they can happen for lots of reasons. Coping with accidents can be frustrating but dealing with them calmly will help prevent them becoming an issue, for you and your toddler.

How to react

Your toddler is bound to have accidents while he's learning to be dry – and even once he's consistently using the potty there will be times when he'll wet himself. How you react, however, will have a big impact on your toddler.

Of course, if your toddler is all dressed up ready to go to a party and suddenly a river starts flowing down his legs, keeping your cool may be a bigger challenge than when an accident happens just before bath time. But the more calm and relaxed you can be, the less threatened your toddler will feel by his mistakes – and the more confidence he will then have that another time he will be able to get it right.

Dos and don'ts when accidents happen

- **Do** commiserate – wet pants are uncomfortable and even embarrassing for your toddler.
- **Do** be matter of fact – simply say "Let's get some dry pants and next time you can try to remember to use your potty."

- **Do** clear up without commenting – keep a bucket and cloth handy.
- **Do** keep on trying – sometimes it may feel that potty training is going on forever and lots of parents wonder if they'll ever see an end to nappies. But all toddlers get there in the end, and staying positive throughout will help give your toddler the confidence he needs to succeed.
- **Don't** make a fuss – remember that accidents are as inevitable as falling over when learning to walk.

My toddler can use the potty but she still wets herself. Why is this?

Almost all toddlers will have several accidents before they become completely dry during the day – after all, their muscles have only just developed enough to allow them to have any control at all over their bowel and bladder, and it will be quite a while yet before they are able to hang on indefinitely.

Possible causes of accidents

If your toddler has very frequent accidents, it may be that she just isn't ready to use the potty yet, in which case it's best to go back to nappies for a couple more weeks before trying again. Often though, accidents happen for other, more everyday reasons – and dealing with these can help you put potty training back on the fast track.

★ **Tiredness** When your toddler is in need of a sleep she'll be less aware that she needs the potty – and less able to hang on. Make sure she doesn't miss her naps.

★ **Slowness** Some toddlers wait until the last minute before looking for the potty – again, occasional reminders from you will help.

COPING WITH ACCIDENTS
There are many everyday reasons why accidents happen. Clearing up quickly and calmly, and offering reassurance when they do occur, will help keep your child's potty training on track.

★ **Nervousness or excitement** If your toddler is overwhelmed by something or coping with a new situation she may lose control of her bladder. Birthday parties or weekends away are common occasions for accidents to happen.

★ **Concentration** When your toddler is deeply absorbed in an activity she'll be more prone to accidents - stay close by so you can remind her to use the potty if necessary.

★ **Lack of coordination** Struggling with pants or trousers can result in last-minute accidents. Always be on hand in case help is needed, and check your toddler is wearing clothes which are easy to remove.

★ **Pressure** Independent-minded toddlers may choose not to use the potty if you push too hard and make too big an issue of it.

★ **Stress** Any big change in your toddler's life – such as the arrival of a baby brother or sister, moving house, a new childminder or starting at playgroup – may cause a temporary setback in using the potty.

IN NEED OF A NAP
Accidents are sometimes more common when your child is tired and in need of sleep – keep an eye on the clock and make sure she doesn't miss her daytime naps.

Bowel accidents

These can happen for all the same reasons as wetting accidents. Sometimes loose stools or constipation can also make it hard for a toddler to control herself.

★ **Loose stools** Your toddler will be less aware that she needs the potty if her stools are soft, which can happen if she is unwell, or eating more fibre or drinking more fruit juice than usual.

★ **Constipation** If your toddler is constipated (see page 43), bowel movements can be painful. This may encourage her to hang on until she just can't wait any more and the movement comes when she's least expecting it.

BUSY DAYS
There may be times when your toddler is so engrossed in what she's doing that she'll forget to go to the toilet.

- **Don't** punish your toddler – getting cross, demanding an apology or looking for a confession will frighten him and delay his progress.
- **Don't** leave him in wet pants – trying to teach him a lesson by not changing him will upset and humiliate him.
- **Don't** tell him he's a baby – this won't encourage grown-up behaviour.

"I'm a big boy now"

Once your toddler is happy on the potty he may want to start using the toilet. Making the toilet a comfortable and safe place to be will help with the transition. Some children, however, develop fears about going to the loo (see page 42). Helping your toddler overcome any worries he has may take time and patience, but your loving support and understanding will help motivate him to try to use the toilet.

Getting used to the toilet is especially useful for when you are out and about (see pages 46–51), and it is necessary if your toddler is going to be starting nursery school soon. He will feel a lot safer if you put a child-sized toilet seat on the usual seat for him to sit on – and he'll need a sturdy stool or box so he can climb up and down by

❝ Charlotte has been dry for months, but she still has the odd accident. When I ask her what happened she says 'I forgot!' I think she sometimes just gets so absorbed in what she's doing she does genuinely 'forget'. ❞

DENISE, mum to Charlotte, aged three years and three months

Expert tip

If your toddler has an accident on the carpet or furniture it's best to deal with it as quickly as possible. After sorting your toddler into dry, clean pants, flush any poo down the toilet then sponge carpets or sofas with cold water. Working from the centre out will help avoid a water stain. If necessary, use some carpet or upholstery shampoo.

himself (see page 19). This will also provide a surface for him to put his feet on when he's sitting on the toilet. Make sure he can reach the loo paper and encourage him to stand on the stool when he has finished so he can wash his hands at the sink, too.

Tips for boys

To begin with your son may be happier sitting on the toilet to wee – many boys take a while to get used to standing up. At some point, however, he'll want to be like his daddy or the other boys at playgroup. Help him along by:
• checking that the loo seat will stay in a raised position – if it falls your child will get a fright and possibly a nasty injury
• teaching him to raise the loo seat when he needs a wee and to put it down afterwards

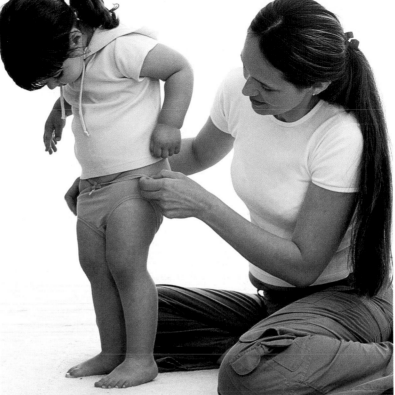

QUICK CHANGE
When accidents occur, change your toddler into dry clothes quickly and calmly.

Urinary tract infections

Sometimes children have repeated accidents because of a medical problem such as a urinary tract infection. These are more common in girls than boys and make bladder control very difficult. If your toddler is keen to use the potty but seems unable to "hang on", or has been dry for a while and then starts having accidents again this may be the cause. Often there are no symptoms, although sometimes your toddler may have:
• a fever
• pain when weeing
• blood in the urine.

Urinary tract infections need medical attention so you should take your child to see your doctor as soon as possible if you are at all concerned.

TEMPTING HIM ONTO THE TOILET
If your child seems concerned about using the toilet, offer lots of encouragement until he feels ready to give it a try.

● offering target practise – put some loo paper "boats" in the loo and get him to try to "sink" them: this will help him perfect his aim

● keeping a cloth and cleaner handy – while he's practising, be prepared for unexpected splashes.

Toilet fears

● "I don't like the toilet"
Some children take a lot longer than others to feel comfortable using the toilet (long after they are dry and clean) and will use one only if there is absolutely no other choice – for example, at someone else's house. It won't do any harm for your toddler to carry on using the potty for now – and in time he'll realize that everyone else uses the toilet safely and happily so there's no reason why he shouldn't too. Meanwhile, offer him lots of encouragement, let him see you and your partner using the toilet, and, when he wants to try, make

sure you are nearby with words
of reassurance.

● **"I don't want to stand up"**
If your son isn't interested in
standing at the loo, don't worry –
let him sit down until he feels ready
to try standing. There's no hurry,
and putting him under pressure
will only make him feel anxious.

● **"I'm scared of the noise"**
Fear of flushing may put your
toddler off using the toilet. Don't
force him to watch or listen to the
flush as this may make his fear
worse. Instead, let him leave the
bathroom first. Then build up his
confidence gradually – start by
flushing the toilet when he's in ear
shot but not in the room; then
encourage him to stand in the
doorway while you flush; finally,
hold his hand or give him a

TAKE A SEAT
*It's fine for your son to
sit down to wee if he
prefers, until he feels
he's ready to try doing
it standing up.*

Constipation and how to deal with it

Constipation can develop for
a number of different reasons,
including:

● too much pressure to perform
during potty training

● fear of using the toilet – especially
when away from home.

What happens
The longer your toddler fails to
have a poo, the harder and drier it
becomes. Having a bowel movement
is then difficult and painful – which
can put your toddler off going again.

What to do
Usually diet and lifestyle changes can
solve the problem. Make sure your
toddler is getting plenty of fibre in his
diet – especially fresh and dried fruit
(raisins, prunes and apricots). Check
that he's drinking lots of fluid –
especially fruit juice – and take him
outside every day for fresh air and
exercise. A little Vaseline at his bowel
opening may also help ease the
movement. Never give your child
laxatives unless recommended by
your doctor.

When to see the doctor
If your toddler doesn't have a bowel
movement for four or five days; if
he has abdominal pain or vomiting;
or if the above methods don't work,
your toddler may need medical help.

Progress seems to be slow. Will my daughter ever be out of nappies?

If your toddler is taking potty training slowly, you may wonder whether she'll ever be out of nappies. You may even start to feel anxious or irritated by her lack of progress, especially if you see other children cottoning on earlier and faster. As with all skills, however, children go at their own pace - and they all get there in the end, even when it comes to potty training.

Staying positive

Don't let your feelings about your toddler's progress – or lack of it – affect your relationship with her. You can't force her to use the potty – after all, only she can control her bladder and her bowel. Instead:

★ remember that potty training isn't a race – comparing your toddler with others is unfair

★ accept that accidents are normal – even toddlers who've used the potty successfully for months make mistakes now and again

★ don't let it dent your confidence – your daughter's potty training is no reflection on your ability as a parent

★ ignore other people's comments – if necessary, explain that your daughter is going at her own pace and you have every confidence she'll get there

★ hide your true feelings – even when it's hard not to feel concerned or unhappy, don't show your toddler. Not only will it be dispiriting for her, she may start to depend on your negative feelings as a good way to get more attention.

INDIVIDUAL PROGRESS
Your child will get the hang of potty training when she is ready and not before. If her friends seem to cotton on quicker, be patient and stay positive – she will get there in the end.

cuddle while you flush. Slowly but surely, with your patience and encouragement, he'll realize there is nothing to fear.

● "I want my nappy"

Lots of toddlers are happy to use the potty or toilet for wees but insist on having their nappy on for poos, perhaps because it gives them a feeling of security. The best way to approach this is to do as your toddler asks but, at the same time, let him know that when he's ready he'll be able to manage using the potty or toilet instead. As long as you don't create any pressure, it's likely that your toddler will put aside nappies for good in his own time.

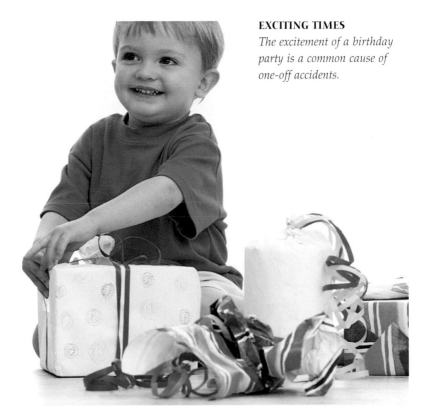

EXCITING TIMES
The excitement of a birthday party is a common cause of one-off accidents.

Questions & Answers

My daughter is two years and two months old and has been dry in the day for quite a few weeks – yet she's still not able to control her bowel. She knows when she's done a poo in her pants – and comes and tells me. I thought children became clean before they became dry?

Your daughter is doing very well if she is already dry as she is still quite young. Try not to worry – in time she will become clean too. Meanwhile, give her lots of praise for all her successes and remind her that she can also use a potty for poos. You can give her a helping hand by keeping an eye on her routine – if she normally needs a poo after lunch or when she wakes up in the morning, watch for the signs and make sure her potty is close by.

At first I tried not to take any notice when Alec wet himself but now I'm beginning to lose my patience. It makes me so cross – especially as he knows how to use the potty. Sometimes I just want to yell at him. What should I do?

Potty training demands lots of patience and sometimes it's hard to be sympathetic, especially if you feel your toddler should know better by now. Maybe you think he's being stubborn, or getting at you on purpose. Or you might be worried that he's taking a long time to get dry – especially compared with your friends' toddlers. Trying to cover up negative feelings can sometimes create extra pressure. Instead, rather than showing your toddler how you feel by yelling at him, tell him how you feel: "Mummy's cross today because she's had to do lots of wiping up." Your toddler needs to know that wet or dirty pants aren't a good thing – but he shouldn't be made to feel that he's a bad boy himself.

" I took a potty **everywhere** with me until my daughter was three. Most people who saw her using it in a car park or down a side street merely **smiled** or looked the other way! "

JACKIE, mum to Jocelyn aged three

5

Out and about

Most toddlers have accidents while being potty trained - which may make the prospect of trips out pretty daunting. But worries about mishaps shouldn't stop you from taking your toddler shopping, round to see friends or away on holiday. As long as you plan ahead, visits - long or short - can still be fun and hassle-free.

Planning ahead

Unless your toddler mastered the art of using a potty in a couple of days, at some point in the early stages of potty training you will have to leave the house, which means closing the front door on your nearest potty and toilet. There may be occasions in the very early days – such as a long car journey – when you feel it's best to put your toddler back in nappies, but a little preparation should make everyday outings go smoothly.

It's best to set out expecting an accident rather than crossing your fingers and hoping it won't happen. Without a travel potty to hand or at least a change of clothes and some idea of where the nearest public loo is, you may find you need to turn round and head home because of wet pants before you've even reached your destination.

Taking a potty out with you is useful with young toddlers, but as they get older you may find they prefer not to do something private in public places! Getting your child familiar with different types of toilets as early as possible will help when you are out and about. And for those times when there's only a nearby tree or bush to hide behind, feeling comfortable about weeing outdoors can save the day.

Travelling long distances

Until your toddler is 100 per cent reliable, travelling could make holidays more challenging.

- Airports, airplanes, trains and train stations have toilets – ask to jump the queue rather than put your toddler at risk of having an accident.
- On long car journeys plan breaks so your toddler can visit a toilet at regular intervals.
- Avoid giving your child fizzy drinks which could stimulate her bladder and make her wee more frequently.

Travel potties

One of the best options when you are stepping out of the front door with your potty-training toddler in tow is to take a travel potty with you. Different types available include:

- those which fold flat yet can be opened in seconds – they are used with absorbent liners which are leak-proof and airtight to prevent spills and smells

- a simple lidded version – ideal for older children who have graduated to using the toilet; you can also invest in a portable toilet seat which is useful for holidays.

I'm worried about going shopping. What do I do if my son needs the loo?

It's a good idea to be home-based for the first few stages of potty training, but for practical as well as social reasons there will come a time when you need to take your toddler out. Leaving the safety of your home can be a worry but, as long as you are prepared, there are lots of ways you can help your son when he needs the toilet.

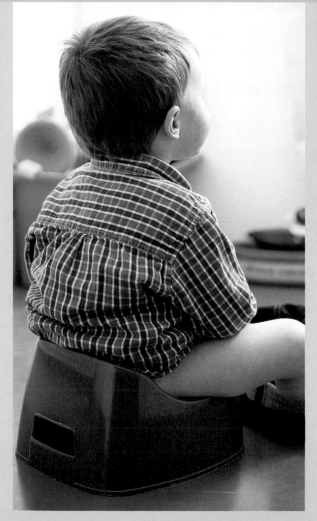

Tips for trouble-free outings

Taking your toddler out and about while potty training means planning ahead – and not being embarrassed when nature calls!

★ Take a potty with you – you can use it in the car, at the park or down a quiet side street.

★ Pack a spare change of clothes – remember that your toddler's outer wear will probably also be wet, so take spare trousers or a skirt as well as pants.

★ Keep a pack of baby wipes handy just in case you are faced with a major clean up.

★ Protect the car and/or buggy seat with a folded towel or plastic bag.

★ Encourage your toddler to use the potty just before you go out, but if he doesn't want to, or he tries but nothing happens, leave it at that.

BEFORE YOU GO OUT
Note when your toddler last used his potty before going shopping, and encourage him to sit on it again just before you go out. This way you will have a sense of when he might need it again.

★ Make a mental note of where the nearest public loo is, so if he needs one you'll know exactly where to head.

★ Note when he last used his potty so you have a sense of when he'll need to use it again.

If nature calls

★ React as quickly as possible, however inconvenient the situation.

★ If you don't have a potty with you or you are some distance from a public toilet, pop into the nearest café or restaurant – even if you are not a customer it's likely that they will let your child use the toilet.

★ Don't be embarrassed about jumping the queue - explain briefly that your toddler can't hang on and most people will smile and let you go to the front.

★ If you are in a shop ask for directions to the nearest loo or, if you have a potty with you, take your toddler to the back of the shop to use it.

★ At the bank, an office or library ask if you can use the staff loo.

★ If you are out in the park, nip behind a tree with your toddler.

★ If your toddler wets his pants - or worse - stay calm. Take him somewhere private so you can clean him up and change him.

PLAN AHEAD
When you are taking your toddler out shopping, make sure you know where the nearest public toilet is so you can get there quickly should the need arise.

BE PREPARED *Make sure you have everything you need – spare clothes, wipes, tissues – close to hand when you go out with your nappy-free toddler.*

• Beakers of juice may help keep your child quiet on a long journey, but bear in mind that drinking lots of fluid while you are travelling will also make her need the toilet more frequently.

• Keep toilet paper and toilet wipes handy – in your bag or in a pocket in the car rather than at the bottom of a suitcase.

Away from home

Some toddlers find unfamiliar places unsettling and may even regress in their potty training. This might be because they feel disorientated, or the loo isn't like the one at home. Overcome any setbacks by:

• taking a potty with you – don't use a holiday as a chance to get her used to using a loo instead

• if she has already progressed to the toilet, take your child's toilet seat cover with you

" I encouraged Gemma to use the toilet from early on and she loved feeling 'grown-up'. This has made outings much easier as she's happy to use a public toilet – checking them out in restaurants or department stores has become one of her favourite pastimes!"

SALLY, mum to Gemma now three and a half

- accept that she may want you to stay with her when she uses the toilet.

Weeing outdoors

There will be times when there's not a loo in sight and your child has no choice but to wee outdoors – whether it's when you are enjoying a family picnic and there are only trees nearby or you are travelling in the car across country and the lay-by will have to do.

With boys it helps if they are already used to weeing standing up – watching daddy can help encourage your son to learn this skill (see also page 41).

HANDY EXTRAS
Travel potties with absorbent liners can be useful when you are between destinations.

For girls it's a little more tricky – you can help by supporting your daughter in a squatting position, or if she's keen to manage on her own, make sure she takes off her pants first, as holding her clothing out of the way so it stays dry will be hard.

ON THE ROAD
If your child needs the loo when she's in the car, stop for her as soon as you can.

Questions & Answers

My husband is taking our three-year-old daughter to visit his parents and he's worried about the toilet facilities at the motorway service station. Will he have to take her into the men's toilet?
At this age, children should always be accompanied when they go to a public toilet. But while it's acceptable for both boys and girls to go into a woman's toilet with their mother or female carer, and for little boys to go with their father into the men's, dads can find it hard when they are out and about with their daughters. Fortunately, many family restaurant chains – including those at motorway service stations – provide "parent and child" facilities which your husband could use. Alternatively, there is often a toilet provided for people with special needs which both men and women can use. You can check toilet facilities on the motorway with an automobile association.

When we are out and about, my five year old will hang on until we get home rather than use a strange toilet. How can I help him feel happy about using a toilet other than his own?
It's very common for young children to feel uncomfortable in an unknown toilet – and, as they get older, they often become concerned about lack of privacy or accidentally locking themselves in. Many public toilets – including school toilets – can also be smelly and off-putting. But "hanging on" for long periods could cause constipation as well as being very uncomfortable. Try to get your son used to other toilets by visiting lots of different ones together – when you are at friends' houses, on a shopping trip or at the local swimming pool, for example. Initially he doesn't need to use one – just let him look. Then, if he's happy to use the toilet, stay with him. Gradually he'll get used to different standards of hygiene, types of flushes and types of door locks until he's confident to use toilets other than his own.

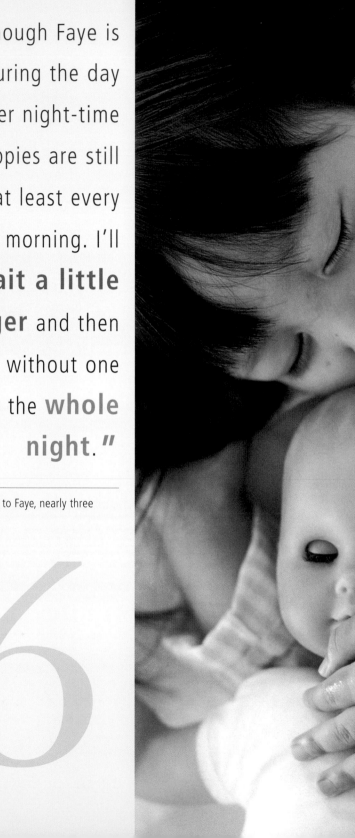

" Although Faye is dry during the day her night-time nappies are still wet at least every other morning. I'll **wait a little longer** and then try her without one for the **whole night**. "

HELENA, mum to Faye, nearly three

6

Dry at night

Your clever toddler is now dry during the day – and both of you are enjoying the freedom of life without nappies. For a while, as his bladder is still maturing, he'll continue to need nappies at night. But watch out for the signs, and at some point before his fourth birthday he'll be ready to be nappy-free at night, too.

Next step forward

For your toddler, staying dry while asleep demands more control than staying dry when awake. Some children still need nappies for daytime naps even if they are otherwise dry. As time goes on, however, and his bladder's capacity grows and strengthens, your child will reach the stage when he can go the whole night without needing a wee - or at least wake up and use the loo or the potty when he feels the urge.

Some toddlers decide nappies are babyish and choose on their own to give them up. With others it's simply a question of watching for the signs that your child is capable of managing without them. Most children are dry at night by the time they are four.

It is likely that, as with daytime dryness, there will be accidents all along the way. Preparing the bed with a waterproof mattress cover and keeping dry nightwear and sheets to hand will help you and your child get back to sleep again quickly. If accidents are still persisting once your child is at school, don't worry - there's lots you can do to help him become dry.

Is he ready?

Just because he's dry during the day doesn't mean your child will automatically become dry at night. Although your toddler can "hang on" during the day before needing to use his potty, holding his urine during the night is a different matter altogether. This is because he sleeps for a long time - hanging on for 10-12 hours requires a strong bladder - and is unable to respond to the bladder's signal that it is full. Until his bladder matures further he will continue to wee during the night - blissfully unaware of what's happening. It's unlikely that your child's bladder will reach the required level of maturity for a while yet.

Expert tip

Look out for "child-size" nappies in your local supermarket – these are ideal for larger toddlers or young children who may have grown out of standard-sized nappies but still need nappies at night.

But how do you know when he is ready to leave off his night-time nappies? Some toddlers, usually the older ones, decide for themselves - although this doesn't necessarily mean they can last until morning without needing a wee.

Avoid ditching the nappies too soon by looking out for the following signs:
• he regularly wakes up with a dry nappy
• he can go three or four hours during the day without a wee
• occasionally he wakes up during the night because he needs a wee.

My son is out of daytime nappies now. When will he be dry at night?

Once your toddler is happily out of nappies during the day, the next big step is becoming dry at night. This may seem like an impossible achievement right now, but when he's developmentally ready, your son will be able to hang on until morning, and give up night-time nappies, too.

What to expect

Although a few toddlers automatically become dry at night once they've mastered daytime control, most still wear a nappy at night for some time afterwards. If your toddler is still having a wee every couple of hours during the day and always wakes up in the morning with a wet nappy, it's likely he'll wet the bed if you take a chance and try him at night-time without a nappy.

Moving towards dryness

As you can't teach your son to hang on until morning - this can only happen with greater maturity of his bladder - there's little you can do to hurry progress along. Instead, watch out for the signs that he is moving towards dryness (see page 53) and avoid putting on any pressure which may make him anxious. He will probably be dry all night by the time he is four, but it's worth bearing in mind that many five year olds are still not 100 per cent dry.

SWEET DREAMS
Don't make an issue out of your toddler becoming dry at night as this could make him anxious – night-time dryness will happen as soon as his bladder is mature enough.

Nights without nappies

Once your child is ready to go without night-time nappies there are ways you can help him become dry at night:

• check that he's happy to sleep without his nappy – as with daytime training, he needs to be emotionally as well as physically ready

• explain to your child that there is a waterproof cover on the bed so that it doesn't matter if he accidentally does a wee in the night

• put a potty nearby in case he wakes up before morning needing a wee

• install a night light in his room so he can see what he is doing if he does wake up and needs the potty

• let him know that he can call you if he wants to – being awake at night can be frightening for small children, and your toddler is more likely to

Expert tip

Wetting accidents will soak right through your child's mattress making it hard to dry – and harder still to remove the smell. Instead, before he goes nappy-free for the night, protect your child's bed with a full-size waterproof sheet or mattress cover under the bottom sheet and tell him that it's there.

TAKING PRECAUTIONS
Talk to your child about not wearing a nappy at night and show him that you are putting a waterproof cover on his mattress so that, if an accident should occur, it doesn't matter.

use the potty in time if he knows
you are on hand to help

● encourage him to remember to
have a wee before he settles down
for the night.

Dealing with accidents

Initially your child will have
accidents at night, especially if you
have a boy. This may happen as
often as two or three times a week
to begin with, becoming less frequent
over the following months until, by
the time he is five, bedwetting is a
thing of the past. Until this age,
accidents should be seen as natural
and unimportant. The best way to
deal with them is to:

● stay calm and matter of fact – if
your child sees that you are upset or
worried it may make him anxious,
which could itself affect his ability to
control his bladder during the night

● keep a pair of dry pyjamas and a
spare sheet close to hand so that
you can change your child and the
bed with the minimum of fuss

● reassure him that this is a phase
that he'll soon grow out of and he
will probably soon become dry of
his own accord.

When he isn't interested

Some children are quite happy to
carry on wetting their night-time
nappies, especially if their parents

*" George was still wearing a nappy at
night when he turned four. I suggested he
tried a night nappy-free and promised
him a special treat if he could do it. It took
a few nights before his first success but
after a couple of weeks he was dry, and
hasn't had an accident since. "*

DOROTHY, mum to George, now five

don't object. Others are afraid of wetting their beds and don't have the confidence to go a night without nappies. If you think your child could manage a dry night, you may need to offer some special motivation.

You could, for example, promise him a special treat for trying. It's important, however, to emphasize the fact that it doesn't matter if the bed does get wet – and that he can always try again the following night. New pyjamas or bed linen may help him feel grown-up, but reassure him that everything can be washed so that he doesn't become concerned about spoiling his nice new things.

Stress and bedwetting

Sometimes a child who was previously dry may start wetting the bed as a reaction to stress. A number of reasons could account for this including, for example, the arrival of a new baby in the family, moving house or a stay in hospital.

If it's easy to spot the reasons for the bedwetting, some special attention and lots of reassurance should help – although it may be a little while before it has an effect. If you are unsure as to what the problem might be, try talking to your child's teacher or anyone else

HANDY POTTY
Leaving a night light on and putting a potty by your child's bed will reassure her and help ease her towards dryness at night.

who helps with his care as they might have a sense of what is bothering your child and how he can be helped.

Older bedwetting

Some children who are over five years of age continue to wet their beds. In medical terms this is known as nocturnal (night-time) enuresis or bedwetting, and affects about one in six five year olds. It's usually boys who are affected and there is often a family history of bedwetting.

If your child is over five and wets the bed frequently, it may be worth seeing your doctor to rule out

problems such as a urinary tract infection, which can be treated with antibiotics. Usually, however, older bedwetting is caused by slow development of the full-bladder response and resolves itself by the time the child is seven years old.

Older children can wear night-time protection pants if they are embarrassed about wearing pull-ups or nappies. These pants look and feel like normal underwear but are also absorbent. Children can put them on themselves which makes them ideal for sleepovers with friends. For more information, contact the Enuresis Resource and Information Centre (see page 62).

Home treatment

There are many things you can do to reassure your child and help him gain night-time control.

• Tell him that you understand and you know it's not his fault.

• If your child is in the habit of having a bedtime drink, make sure it isn't a large amount of fluid.

WAKING UP TO WEE
If your older child is struggling to gain night-time control, encouraging him to wake up and go to the loo when you are going to bed may help him along the way.

- Make sure he uses the toilet before settling down for the night.
- Motivate him with small incentives such as his favourite comic when he has a dry night.
- If your child is older, wake him up to have a wee when you go to bed.

Another measure which can also help is a bedwetting alarm. This is an alarm which goes off each time your child begins to wet the bed, giving him the chance to get up and finish weeing in the loo. It has been shown to be successful with many children and often works especially well in combination with rewards for dry nights. Talk to your health visitor or GP if you think one of these might help.

BEDTIME DRINKS
Having a drink at bedtime should not affect your child's ability to stay dry at night – her bladder's capacity will adjust to the amount of liquid it gets used to.

Questions & Answers

My daughter still drinks a beaker of milk before going to sleep. Should I cut this out to help her stay dry during the night?
It might seem sensible not to give your daughter drinks in the evening as a way of helping her stay dry all night. But you should always let your child drink if she's thirsty – especially as cutting back won't make any difference to her bladder control. If there is less fluid to hold, the bladder adjusts so that it feels as full as it did when it was holding more. And, over a period of time, cutting back on drinks will simply reduce the bladder's capacity – which could make matters worse. Once she has developed enough control to go through the night without wetting the bed it won't matter how much your daughter drinks – but don't let her have fizzy drinks or drinks containing caffeine, such as tea or coffee, as these can stimulate the bladder into action.

My friend wakes her three year old up when she goes to bed at night and puts him on the loo. Is this a good tactic to try?
Many parents do this as a way of avoiding night-time accidents. But while it helps prevent wet sheets it doesn't encourage bladder control. Not only is the child often still half asleep and barely aware of what he is doing, he is also being asked to do the one thing you want to avoid – namely wee during the night! Instead, you want your child to wake when he feels the urge to go or hang on until morning. If "lifting" is the only way to prevent accidents, maybe your child isn't developed enough yet to go a whole night without weeing. This tactic might, however, be useful with an older child – one who is five or six and trying hard to keep dry at night. In this case, make sure he is fully awake so he can sense for himself that he has a full bladder.

Potty training guide

Here's a broad guide to the ages and stages of potty training, what you can expect and what you can do to help your toddler. Remember, as with all developmental milestones, every child will reach the required levels of maturity in his own time.

Baby's age	Your toddler's development	What to expect
up to 18 months	The nerve pathways that connect your baby's bladder and bowel to her brain are not fully matured.	Your baby is still emptying her bowel and bladder automatically as a reflex action, unaware of what is happening.
18 months	The nerve pathways that connect her bladder and bowel to her brain should be fully mature.	Your toddler is starting to develop a level of control over her bowel and bladder movements – her nappies are often dry for a period of time and she is becoming aware of what's happening when she wees or poos.
two to three years	As the bladder and bowel muscles strengthen, the ability to "hang on" increases.	Your child is keen to please, wants to imitate you, can follow simple instructions, is reasonably coordinated and is increasingly eager for independence.
three to five years	Your child's control over her bladder and bowel is sufficient for her to be able to hang on for reasonable periods of time and even wake up at night in response to a full bladder.	Your child is ready to give up nappies at night-time but, again, expect accidents initially.

What you can do

Start to use words such as "wee" and "poo" when you change her nappy; stay matter of fact about dirty nappies, and let her see you and your partner using the toilet.

Introduce your toddler to the potty but don't expect to start potty training yet.

Start potty training – but don't expect too much too soon. Initially there may be lots of accidents.

Stay calm and relaxed to increase your child's confidence that she can get it right. With older children, small incentives can often help.

Useful contacts

British Nutrition Foundation
High Holborn House
52–54 High Holborn
London WC1V 6RQ
Tel: 020 7404 6504
www.nutrition.org.uk
Promoting nutritional wellbeing.

BabyCentre
(Content Consultants)
84 Dereham road
Easton
Norwich NR9 5DF
Tel: 01603 882129
www.babycentre.co.uk
Provides information, support and
guidance on all parenting issues.

Contact a Family
209–211 City Road
London EC1V 1JN
Tel: 0808 808 3555
(Mon–Fri, 10am–4pm)
www.cafamily.org.uk
Helping families who care for
children with any disability or
special need.

Council for Disabled Children
8 Wakley Street
London EC1V 7QE
Tel: 020 7843 6000
www.ncb.org.uk
Supporting families with disabled
children.

Down's Syndrome Association
155 Mitcham Road
London SW17 9PG
Tel: 020 8682 4001
www.downs-syndrome.org.uk
Advice on potty training a child
with Down's syndrome.

Enuresis Resource and
Information Centre
34 Old School House
Britannia Road
Kingswood
Bristol BS15 8DB
Helpline: 0117 960 3060
(Mon–Fri, 10am–4pm)
www.enuresis.org.uk
Support and advice on wetting
and soiling.

Community Practitioners and
Health Visitors Association
40 Bermondsey Street
London SE1 3UD
Tel: 020 7939 7000
www.msfcphva.org
Advice and information on potty
training your child.

National Autistic Society
393 City Road
London EC1V 1NG
Tel: 020 7833 2299
www.nas.org.uk
Advice on potty training a child
with autism.

National Childbirth Trust
Alexandra House
Oldham Terrace
Acton
London W3 6NH
Tel: 0870 4448707
www.nctpregnancyandbabycare.com
Support and information on potty
training your child.

Parentline Plus
520 Highgate Studios
53–79 Highgate Road
London NW5 1TL
Tel: 0808 800 2222
www.parentlineplus.org.uk
Support and information for parents.

NHS Direct
Tel: 0845 4647
www.nhsdirect.nhs.uk
Health information on the internet.

TAMBA (Twins and Multiple
Birth Association)
2 The Willows
Gardner Road
Guildford
Surrey GU1 4PG
Tel: 0870 770 3305
www.tamba.org.uk
Advice on potty training twins
or more.

Index

Acknowledgments

Dorling Kindersley would like to thank Sally Smallwood and Ruth Jenkinson for the photography, and Sue Bosanko for compiling the index.

Models Rachana and Arianne Shah, David with Maya Bowles, Naginder with Gobind Jahal, Lily Rose Spick, Jo with Jade Sollinger, Thompson family, Isaac Clyne, Ivor with Ruby Baddiel, Thea Collins, Sharon with Marcus Gunn, Paul with Oscar Ford, Aimee Morland, Jenny with Baobao Cao, Nicolette with Marta Comand, Reilly family, Ria Shah, Mark with Sophira Norr, Maureen and Janis Lopatkin with Mia Schindler, Harvey Barron, Lucas Mtfolo, Tom Orchard, Lou-Fong family.

Hair and make-up Victoria Barnes, Louise Heywood, Susie Kennett, Amanda Clarke

Picture researcher Anna Bedewell

Picture librarian Romaine Werblow

Picture credits
Dorling Kindersley would like to thank the following for their kind permission to reproduce their photographs:
14: ImageState/Pictor: Robert Llewellyn; 15: Getty Images: Britt Erlanson.

All other images © Dorling Kindersley. For further information see: www.dkimages.com